ALL AROUND THE WORLD
GUATEMALA

by Joanne Mattern

pogo

Ideas for Parents and Teachers

Pogo Books let children practice reading informational text while introducing them to nonfiction features such as headings, labels, sidebars, maps, and diagrams, as well as a table of contents, glossary, and index.

Carefully leveled text with a strong photo match offers early fluent readers the support they need to succeed.

Before Reading

- "Walk" through the book and point out the various nonfiction features. Ask the student what purpose each feature serves.
- Look at the glossary together. Read and discuss the words.

Read the Book

- Have the child read the book independently.
- Invite him or her to list questions that arise from reading.

After Reading

- Discuss the child's questions. Talk about how he or she might find answers to those questions.
- Prompt the child to think more. Ask: The patterns on the clothing in Guatemala show others where they are from. Can others tell where you are from by looking at your clothing?

Pogo Books are published by Jump!
5357 Penn Avenue South
Minneapolis, MN 55419
www.jumplibrary.com

Library of Congress Cataloging-in-Publication Data

Names: Mattern, Joanne, 1963- author.
Title: Guatemala : all around the world / by Joanne Mattern.
Description: Minneapolis, MN : Jump!, Inc., 2019.
Series: All around the world | "Pogo Books."
Includes index.
Identifiers: LCCN 2018018393 (print)
LCCN 2018020423 (ebook)
ISBN 9781641281638 (ebook)
ISBN 9781641281614 (hardcover : alk. paper)
ISBN 9781641281621 (pbk.)
Subjects: LCSH: Guatemala—Juvenile literature.
Classification: LCC F1463.2 (ebook)
LCC F1463.2 .M38 2019 (print) | DDC 972.81—dc23
LC record available at https://lccn.loc.gov/2018018393

Editor: Kristine Spanier
Designer: Molly Ballanger

Photo Credits: Diego Grandi/Shutterstock, cover, 11; Tati Nova photo/Shutterstock, 1; Pixfiction/Shutterstock, 3; robertharding/Superstock, 4; Byron Ortiz/Shutterstock, 5; Ben Pipe Photography/Getty, 6-7; Ondrej Prosicky/Shutterstock, 8-9tl; Vladimir Wrangel/Shutterstock, 8-9tr; Adalbert Dragon/Shutterstock, 8-9bl; Christian Musat/Shutterstock, 8-9br; Rob Crandall/Shutterstock, 10; ton koene/Alamy, 12-13; Matyas Rehak/Shutterstock, 14-15; montree imnam/Shutterstock, 15(sugarcane); Fanfo/Shutterstock, 16; Oksana Mizina/Shutterstock, 17; Aleksandar Todorovic/Shutterstock, 18-19; Lucy Brown - loca4motion/Shutterstock, 20-21; Anton_Ivanov/Shutterstock, 23.

Printed in the United States of America at Corporate Graphics in North Mankato, Minnesota.

TABLE OF CONTENTS

CHAPTER 1

WELCOME TO GUATEMALA!

Spy the rare quetzal in a rain forest. Gaze at crumbling **temples**. Wander through the bright colors of a market. Welcome to Guatemala!

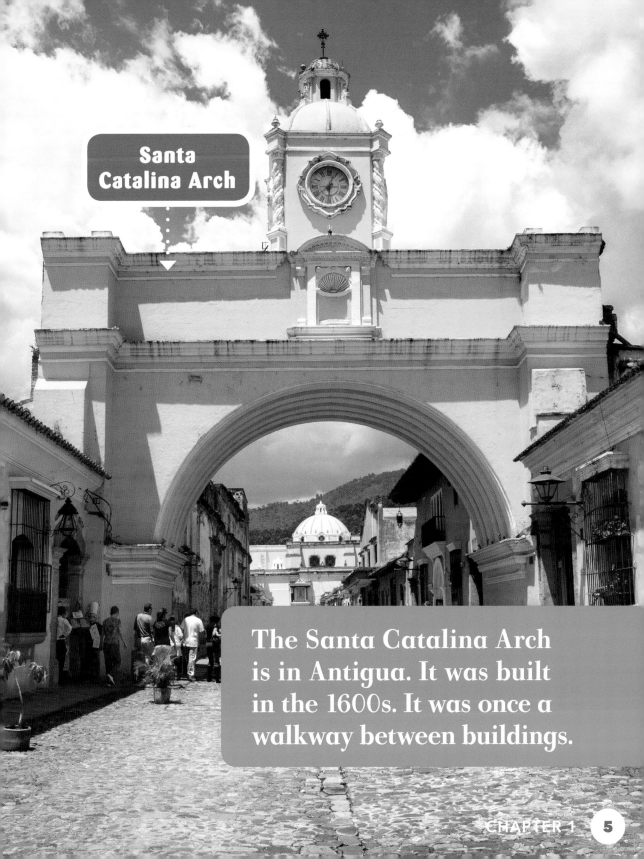

Santa Catalina Arch

The Santa Catalina Arch is in Antigua. It was built in the 1600s. It was once a walkway between buildings.

You will find 37 **volcanoes** throughout the land here. Some are still active! Visitors can hike to the top of Pacaya Volcano. Here you may see hot ash and lava up close.

DID YOU KNOW?

The steam from beneath Pacaya Volcano heats the surrounding rock. Hikers bring marshmallows to roast!

Pacaya Volcano

lava

quetzal

loggerhead sea turtle

jaguar

anteater

The country is filled with amazing animals. The quetzal is one of 900 kinds of birds here. There are 200 kinds of **reptiles**. The loggerhead sea turtle is one. Jaguars and pumas prowl through the forests. Monkeys and anteaters are here, too.

CHAPTER 2

LIFE IN GUATEMALA

The Mayan **Empire** once ruled this land. Tikal National Park is filled with Mayan **ruins**. Many temples are here! When were they built? More than 900 years ago!

temple

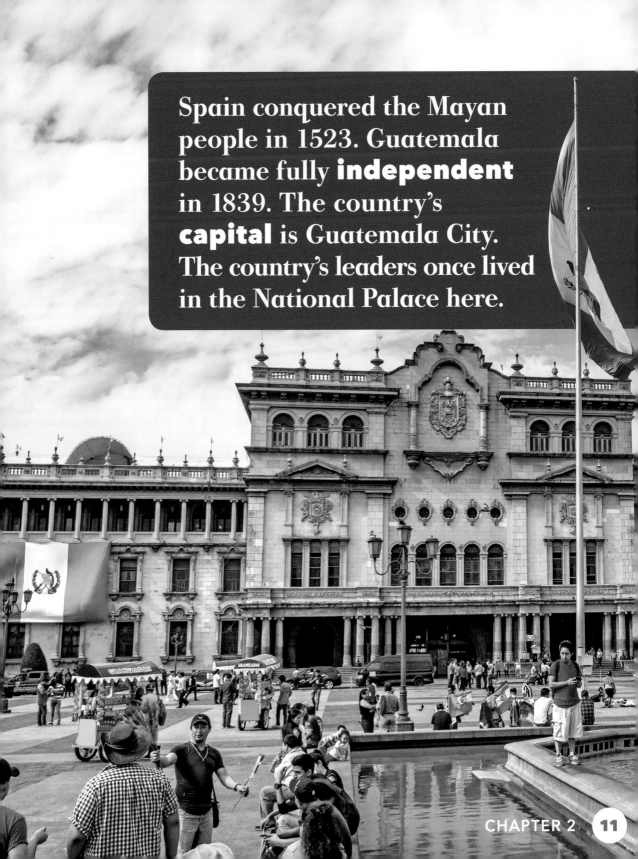

Spain conquered the Mayan people in 1523. Guatemala became fully **independent** in 1839. The country's **capital** is Guatemala City. The country's leaders once lived in the National Palace here.

Some schools have just one or two rooms for all of the students. Often there are not enough desks or supplies. Students may end their education before high school. Why? To help their families. Or to earn money. Those who stay in school focus on training for jobs.

WHAT DO YOU THINK?

Students of all ages may learn together in the same room. Would you like this? Why or why not?

Buses are used for transportation here. They are school buses from the United States. Each one is painted in different bright colors.

People may ride the buses to their jobs. Many people work on farms. **Crops** here are coffee. Sugarcane. Corn. Bananas.

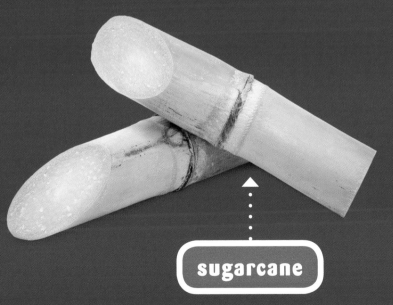

sugarcane

CHAPTER 3

GUATEMALA'S PEOPLE

What is for dinner? Try chicken pepian. This is chicken with a spicy pumpkin and sesame sauce. It is served with rice. Yum!

Horchata is a popular drink. It is cold milk mixed with rice and sugar. Cocoa and cinnamon flavor it.

horchata

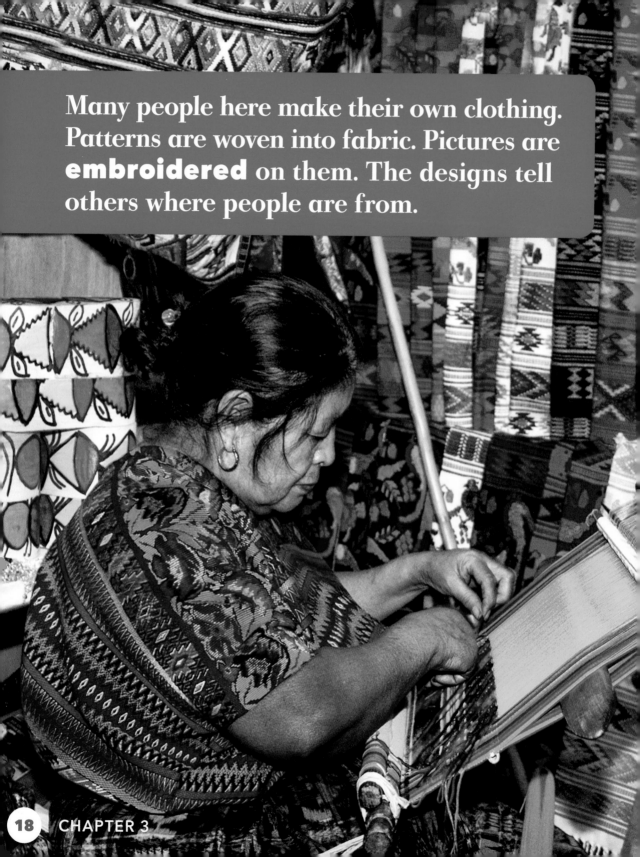

Many people here make their own clothing. Patterns are woven into fabric. Pictures are **embroidered** on them. The designs tell others where people are from.

TAKE A LOOK!

Traditional Mayan clothing is an important part of the **culture** here. These outfits have many pieces to them.

CINTA
(hair ribbon)

SOMBRERO
(hat)

HUIPIL
(blouse)

REBOZO
(shawl)

CAPIXAY
(overshirt)

FAJA
(sash)

CINTURÓN
(belt)

FALDA
(skirt)

BOLSA
(bag)

PANTALÓN
(pants)

SANDALIAS
(sandals)

Easter is an important holiday here. Large parades take place this week. Colorful carpets are created on the streets before parades. What are they made of? Sawdust and flowers! **Stencils** are used to create the designs.

This is a country full of color. What an amazing place!

WHAT DO YOU THINK?

The Christmas season here begins on December 7. Families clean their homes on this date to prepare for the holiday. How does your family prepare for a big holiday?

stencil

AT A GLANCE

MEXICO

BELIZE

Caribbean Sea

GUATEMALA

Guatemala City ★

HONDURAS

EL SALVADOR

Pacific Ocean

N
W ┼ E
S

GUATEMALA

Location: Central America

Size: 42,043 square miles (108,890 square kilometers)

Population: 15,460,732 (July 2017 estimate)

Capital: Guatemala City

Type of Government: presidential republic

Languages: Spanish and Mayan

Exports: clothing, coffee, fruits, petroleum, sugar

Currency: Guatemalan quetzal

GLOSSARY

capital: A city where government leaders meet.

crops: Plants grown for food.

culture: The ideas, customs, traditions, and ways of life of a group of people.

embroidered: To have sewn a picture or a design onto cloth using different colors of thread or yarn.

empire: A group of countries or states that has the same ruler.

independent: Free from a controlling authority.

reptiles: Cold-blooded animals that have dry, scaly skin.

ruins: The remains of something that has collapsed or been destroyed.

stencils: Pieces of paper, plastic, or metal with patterns cut out in order to transfer the designs to surfaces below.

temples: Buildings used for worship.

volcanoes: Mountains with openings through which molten lava, ash, and hot gases erupt.

Guatemala's currency

INDEX

TO LEARN MORE

Learning more is as easy as 1, 2, 3.

1) Go to www.factsurfer.com
2) Enter "Guatemala" into the search box.
3) Click the "Surf" button to see a list of websites.

With factsurfer, finding more information is just a click away.